W0019569

GRIN - Verlag für akademische Texte

Der GRIN Verlag mit Sitz in München hat sich seit der Gründung im Jahr 1998 auf die Veröffentlichung akademischer Texte spezialisiert.

Die Verlagswebseite www.grin.com ist für Studenten, Hochschullehrer und andere Akademiker die ideale Plattform, ihre Fachtexte, Studienarbeiten, Abschlussarbeiten oder Dissertationen einem breiten Publikum zu präsentieren.

Dokument Nr. V22471 aus dem GRIN Verlagsprogramm

Leonhard Stampler

Forgiveness - A review on a new trend of psychological and medical research under theological aspects

GRIN Verlag

Bibliografische Information der Deutschen Nationalbibliothek: Die Deutsche Bibliothek
verzeichnet diese Publikation in der Deutschen Nationalbibliografie; detaillierte bibliografische Daten sind im Internet über http://dnb.d-nb.de/ abrufbar.

1. Auflage 2003
Copyright © 2003 GRIN Verlag
http://www.grin.com/
Druck und Bindung: Books on Demand GmbH, Norderstedt Germany
ISBN 978-3-638-84233-4

Forgiveness
A review on a new trend of
psychological and medical research
under theological aspects

Seminararbeit aus Religionspsychologie
am Institut für Katechetik und Religionspädagogik
der Karl-Franzens-Universität Graz

Leonhard Stampler

1 Introduction

While the concept of forgiveness is known to any Christian in the world, it is new to use this concept within psychology and psychotherapy. Physicians (Phillipps and Osborne, 1989) working with cancer patients and therapists (Kaufman, 1984; Fitzgibbons, 1986; Hope, 1987) who were looking for ways to efficiently reduce anger, recognized the utility of forgiveness.[1] Since the last 20 years some American psychologists, psychotherapists and also medical doctors researched on this subject and many studies could show the effects of forgiving an offender to either mental and physical health.

The forgiveness-research is doubtlessly *auch für die christliche Spiritualität und Verkündigung von Belang*[2], because psychology can show that forgiveness is not only a matter of theological research and that there are other possible motivations to forgive than religious ones.

My work will describe some of the most important psychological studies of forgiveness in relation to mental and physical health. Furthermore I will describe some questions of the Christian community faced by the fact that the central faith proclamation is matter of empirical psychological and medical research.

2 Understandings of the concept of forgiveness

2.1 Psychological definitions of forgiveness[3]

A working definition of forgiveness is the one drawn by J. North (1987) Although the forgiver does not deny himself/herself the moral right to have an resentment toward his/her offender, he overcomes this resentment by trying to feel compassion, benevolence or even love toward the offender, knowing that the latter has definitely no moral right for such a merciful response. The feelings of the forgiver toward his offender are changing in two different aspects: firstly negative feelings are decreasing (like anger, resentment, etc.) and a positive feelings (like compassion, love, etc.) are increasing.

Basing on this premises Enright et al. (1991) expanded the definition as follows: While North is concentrating on the changes of the forgiver's feelings towards the offender, Enright et al.

---

[1] Subkoviak, Michael J. et al: Measuring forgiveness in late adolescence and middle adulthood, in: Journal of Adolescence, 1995, 18, 641
2Grom, B.: Forgiveness: die Bereitschaft zu vergeben. Ein aufstrebendes Thema psychologischer Beratung und Forschung, in: Stimmen der Zeit, 220 (2002), 640-643
[3] Subkoviak, Michael J. et al: Measuring forgiveness in late adolescence and middle adulthood, in: Journal of Adolescence, 1995, 18, 642

also included changes in the judgments (how the forgiver *thinks* about the offender) and the behaviour (how the forgiver *acts* toward the offender) in the forgiving process. Also with judgements and cognitive components (like with feelings) it is possible to note a cessation of negative condemning judgements or negative behaviour (like revenge) and the presence of positive judgements or behaviour (like helpfulness, overtures toward reconciliation). In sum Enright et al. describe forgiveness as a matter including six components:

- Absence of negative affect

- Presence of positive affect

- Absence of negative judgement

- Presence of positive judgement

- Absence of negative behaviour

- Presence of positive behaviour

2.2 Arguments against Forgiveness[4]

In literature you can also find arguments against interpersonal forgiveness: one of this arguments is that forgiving leaves the forgiver open to further abuse. Looking at the definitions above, it's easy to see, that this is an invalid argument. It is a confusion of reconciliation and forgiveness. Forgiveness is one persons stance toward another, whereas reconciliation occurs when two people come together in behavioural way and both parties do their part to respect the other. Though the forgiver can see, that the other shows no sign to offer respect and there's no chance to reconcile, the forgiver can reduce the negative and increase the positive responses toward the other. It's important to say, that forgivers are not blind to the offender's faults, but the forgiver protects himself against hatred and resentment that can increase anxiety or depression widthin oneself, and so forgiveness is in fact a way to protect oneself.

---

[4] Subkoviak, Michael J.: Measuring forgiveness in late adolescence and middle adulthood, in: Journal of Adolescence, 1995, 18, 642-643

2.3 The process of forgiving – a model

It's undisputable in literature that the possibility of forgiving an offender must mature during a process. To describe a general pathway people follow when they forgive someone Robert Enright has developed a model[5] of this process, that has 20 steps which are organised in 4 distinct phases. The steps may be differing from individual to individual, some may experience only some of the steps, some may experience even more steps.
I'll try to give a brief description of the four phases of Enright's concept:

2.3.1 Uncovering Phase

During this phase the individual shall become aware of the emotional pain the offender has caused to him or her in a deep and unjust way. Because of the deep injury the individual may have feelings of anger or even hatred toward the offender. The confrontation with these deep negative emotions might burden the individual seriously. In this phase it will be necessary to decide on an appropriate amount of energy to process this pain but still function effectively. When anger, hatred and all the other negative feelings are brought out into the open, healing can start to occur.

2.3.2 Decision Phase

In this phase the individual shall realize that focussing on the suffered injury and on the injurer will cause more pain to oneself than necessary. Appending the injury is an additional burden and no way to solve the problems. So the individual begins to understand that a change to more positive feelings, judgments and behaviour would be the better way to process the suffered pain. So the individual starts to realize that forgiveness is the best strategy to heal the injury. He/she is not ready to completely forgive his/her offender but he/she has decided to explore forgiveness and to take initial steps toward full forgiveness.

2.3.3 Work Phase

Being in this phase of the process of forgiving the forgiver will start the active work of forgiving. He/she may start to think about different aspects that might have been the reason for the injurers actions. He/she might start to understand that the injurer had a bad childhood and see this as a reason for the injuring actions. He/she might put the injury in context to pressures the injurer had to face when acting so injuriously. It's important to say, that this new way of thinking about the offender is no excusing of the offenders responsibility for the

---

[5] Enright, Robert and Reed, Gale: A process model of forgiving, in: http://www.forgiveness-institute.org/ifi/whatis/process_model_of_forgiving.html (fetched 04 February 2003)

offense(s), but a way to better understand him/her and to see him as a member of human community. This new way of thinking may be connected with the try to feel empathy with the injurer or to feel compassion toward him/her. Also included in this phase is the heart of forgiveness: the forgiver accepts the pain that has resulted from the actions of the injurer That must not to be confused with any sense of deserving the pain. It's only an important step to bearing the pain, and bearing the pain means that the injured person doesn't pass it to other persons, including the injurer. Now the individual may begin to show good will toward the injurer and reconciliation may or may not occur.

2.3.4 Outcome / Deepening phase

In this phase the individual starts to realize that forgiving is an emotional relief to himself/herself and that the pain he/she is suffering has got a meaning. It's paradox but true: by giving the offender mercy, compassion and love the individual helps himself/herself. That's a understanding the forgiver may gain, and through compassion for self and others and active input in the society the forgiver will start to feel a new sense of life.

2.4 Christian understandings

In the Christian religion forgiveness is a central theme. Looking in the Old Testament (We cannot have eternal life and heaven without God's forgiveness: "If You, Lord, should mark iniquities, O Lord, who could stand? But there is forgiveness with You, that You may be feared[6]) and coming to New Testament (e.g. Jesus' command to forgive seventy times seven in Mt:18) forgiveness is at the centre of the gospel message and shape of Christian identity.[7] Forgiveness is at one side a gift of God and on the other side (how it is mentioned in the Lord's Prayer) we should grant forgiveness and we will receive forgiveness granted to us by God. Jesus Christ is an example for Christians in the whole world. He taught us to forgive our offenders and God our father will forgive us our faults. So this is the example Christians should follow. This view of forgiveness shows us that forgiveness will have a positive effect for us and tells us that it is good and right to forgive others. But what the Bible cannot tell us is what is going on within us humans when we forgive and what effect forgiveness has on us and our health! This knowledge is now given to us by the actual empirical psychological and medical research.

---

[6] Ps 130
[7] VanOyen Witvliet, Forgiveness and Health: Review and reflections on a matter of faith, feelings, and physiology, in: Journal of Psychology and Religion, 29 (2001), 213

3 Published Research on Forgiveness and mental and physical health

In this chapter I'd like to describe the actual status of research of forgiveness and health (mental and physical). This description is mainly based on the article of Charlotte vanOyen Witvliet (2001)[8].

3.1 Forgiving and its effect on mental health

In the 1960s J. G. Emerson discovered an association of feeling forgiven and mental well-being, because he found that when people's scores showed a better mental condition scores also showed that they felt a stronger sense of being forgiven. So Emerson found this connection in the 1960s and then three decades nothing happened on this sector of research.

In 1993 Robert Enright and J. H. Hebl published the first in a wave of studies on the matter of forgiveness. They focused on 24 women who were recently hurt painfully. (e.g. children who didn't visit them, marital conflicts, etc.) The women were randomly assigned to a group practicing forgiveness intervention or a control group, which discussed topics raised by its members. Though both groups showed improvements in anxiety and depression scores it was discovered that this improvements and the scores on self-esteem were higher in the forgiveness group, and scores on depression and anxiety were lower in the forgiveness group than in the other group. So the members of the forgiveness group had better mental health in terms of self-esteem, depression and anxiety scores.

In 1996 Enright published together with S.R Freedman a study dealing with forgiveness intervention in cases of incest. The worked with 12 adult women who had survived incest including physical contact by a male relative two or more years ago. The built pairs of women and one of each pair was assigned to the one-on-one treatment and the other to a wait-list control group. Compared to pre-treatment scores the treated women show higher increases in forgiveness and hope and decreases in anxiety and depression than the wait-listed women. When the treatment for the one was over, the other entered the treatment. When they wait-listed women also completed their treatment, they showed similar results. So mental health had improved in both groups.

In 1997 Enright and Coyle used a similar forgiveness intervention working with ten men who felt hurt because their partners decided on an abortion. They were randomly assigned for

---

[8] VanOyen Witvliet, Forgiveness and Health: Review and reflections on a matter of faith, feelings, and physiology, in: Journal of Psychology and Religion, 29 (2001), 214 - 218

forgiveness intervention and wait-listed control group. Also this men improved their mental health during their forgiveness intervention.

This studies are only examples and there are many other studies and not all could find a strong link between forgiveness and mental health, but many of them showed the efficacy of forgiveness intervention in connection with mental health because reducing unforgiveness and forcing forgiveness seem to improve scores on self-esteem, depression and anxiety. These are important factors for being mentally healthy and so I think it's possible to say that forgiveness intervention is able to improve mental health.

3.2 Forgiving and its effect on physical health

Given an increasing evidence of the mind-body connection, it's obvious to suggest that forgiveness effects also on physical health. A few studies examine on forgiveness and physical benefit. Mostly they are focusing primarily on the matter of physical costs caused by unforgiving answers. Mainly the focus is set to hostility and its effect on physical health (e.g. in studies dealing with coronary heart diseases as I'll describe in the following). Forgiveness and hostility have an inverse relationship. If the one goes up, the other goes down and vice versa. So if someone gives forgiving answers to an offender hostility is reduced. However, in matter of coronary heart disease hostility is seen as a risk factor, because highly hostile people seem to be more physiologically reactive to interpersonal offences than low-hostile persons. So highly hostile people experience exaggerated flight-or-flight responses of the sympathetic nervous system (SNS), and this causes an exaggerated release of stress hormones which furthermore can cause coronary heart disease. Another fact why reducing hostility is good for physical well-being is that highly hostile persons tend to engage in more risky behaviours such as smoking or greater consumption of food and alcohol. So hostility is physically dangerous and a risk for heart attacks. Forcing forgiveness in this cases will reduce hostility and this will reduce the risk of heart diseases. In fact forgiveness could be not directly but indirectly a help by treating heart diseases.

Another study on the effect of forgiveness on physical health is the one of Witvliet, Ludwig and Vander Laan (2001). They asked participants to identify a real-life offender and to imagine giving this offender variable positive (forgiving) or negative (unforgiving) responses. By comparing the physiological and emotional responses participants generated when thinking of situations where they could not forgive an offender with responses they generated when imagining situations where they could forgive the offender or were able to feel empathy with him/her they could see the following: During the unforgiving imagery participants

showed greater reactivity in heart rate and blood pressure than in forgiving imageries; the
same held for the sympathetic nervous system and the brow muscles showed a greater tension.
This effects persisted even after the imagery trials in the relaxing period. Participants also
reported that they felt more negative emotion during unforgiving imagery trials than during
forgiving trials, they did feel less stress during the forgiving trials, more positive emotions
and greater perceived control. So it is obvious to suggest that harbouring unforgiving
responses toward an offender leads to mental and physiological costs and by forgiving these
costs will be reduced and this could lead to psycho physiological benefits.

So we can see that forgiveness also has an effect on our body and our physical health. There
are not much studies about this matter but the few studies having examined this forgiveness
and physical health show that forgiving and unforgiving can have either positive or negative
long term effects on health.

4 Reflections on the Christian community

According to Charlottes vanOyen Witvliets article[9] there are five questions Christian
communities have to face when facing the empirical researches on forgiveness matters. I'll
describe in brief this five questions and Witvliets answers, I'll try to establish a relationship
between the considered questions and our lecture on Religionspsychologie and I'll try to
explain my personal point of view considering this questions.

4.1 Empirical research versus theological inquiry

The first question is if empirical research should be used to study forgiveness? On the one
hand Christians might ask, if a deeply Christian rooted matter should be studied by empirical
researchers and on the other hand empirical researchers may ask whether forgiveness is too
spiritual to be appropriate for study? I think as we said in our lecture it would be quite
interesting an important for either theologians and psychologists to have a look on the
respectively other branch of research. As the Bible tells us about Gods grace and Gods
forgiveness and describes models for interpersonal forgiveness, it doesn't tell about the
detailed process going on in our brains and bodies when forgiving a person and also for
theologians the results of the empirical researches will be interesting. The empirical studies
will and shall not displace theologian and philosophic inquiry, its function is to illumine
what's going on within a human who practices forgiveness. The Bible also doesn't negate the
value of other understandings and aspects of the concept of forgiveness and the biblical

---

[9] VanOyen Witvliet, Forgiveness and Health: Review and reflections on a matter of faith, feelings, and
physiology, in: Journal of Psychology and Religion, 29 (2001), 220 - 222

understanding shall be a motivation for us to understand all the aspects of forgiveness either experimental (combined with emotional and physical health effects) and theological aspects. I think it's somehow reductionistic when we focus on one and only one way of understanding problems and processes and I don't think that the intent of the empirical analysis is to understand forgiveness as a construct of natural science and reduce the theological and anthropological meaning. So it may be said that empirical research on forgiveness matters is an enrichment for theological inquiry, an enrichment for the world and a new way to better understand human. It also may be said that the empirical research is no replacement for the concept of forgiveness announced in the Bible but a complement and in my opinion even an affirmation, because it emphasises the importance of being forgiving by understanding it in a new way and being able to give new reasons for being forgiving.

4.2 Empirical research – a new apologetic?

The second questions is whether empirical research should serve as a new apologetic to speak properly to our health-oriented society. This question includes the assumption that empirical research and investigation even have the power to test or prove theological truth claims. Although empirical investigation may offer a way of knowing about forgiving and its effect on our mental and physical health it cannot usurp the role of theology and philosophy. There are many theological and philosophical truth claims that cannot be tested with empirical research. The inquiry of dimensions of reality that are not empirical provable is matter of theology and philosophy and will stay even when empirical researches can tell us something new about things we thought we cannot explain. Furthermore empirical research of forgiveness are not able to tell us why forgiveness exists and why forgiveness has its described effects on our health. It can in fact describe what is going on within our human brains and bodies and it can tell us that forgiveness is a way to escape mental illnesses caused by interpersonal offences and hurts. So it is the role of theology and philosophy trying to explain the origin of forgiveness and asking why it exists. Another reason why empirical forgiveness research may be inappropriate as a Christian apologetic is, that forgiveness is not practiced by Christians only. The data given by the empirical studies includes also data from non-Christian people and forgiving is a matter for a variety of people with very different even religious and non-religious backgrounds. And furthermore it may be that we find that forgiveness is not really more beneficial for health than avoidance, tolerance and other ways to minimize severity of offences but even if studies fail by showing an irrefutable link between forgiveness and health this cannot undermine the truth claims of Christianity. So in my opinion empirical research will not replace the theological inquiry on different matters, it

will not prove or not prove Christian truth claims and so it cannot be a new apologetic replacing the Christian one. Knowing about empirical questions cannot replace our faith in God and in our philosophy of faith, that are two strictly different ways of perceiving reality and both ways together will help us to find the truth.

4.3 Empirical forgiveness research – motivation to forgive?

The third question is whether the results of empirical research shall motivate us to forgive. Shall the motivation to forgive be influenced by the motivation to benefit ourselves? Now it's important to differ between empirical research data and prescriptions or proscriptions of behaviour in relation to this results. Surely some people may only practice forgiveness because of the motivation to benefit themselves, but if they do so they help even their offender and they help that another little step to peace has been done. So I think though the motivations are very self-concentrated the result is a benefit for others to. Surely Christians should forgive because of following the example of Christ and forgiving should be a matter of course to Christians and not based on self-concentrated motivations, but can the motivation to forgive an other person be seen only as self-concentrated? Isn't forgiving the other besides self-benefit also a benefit for the other(s)? And why not doing something for another person knowing and enjoying that it is something I do also for myself? The data of empirical research may augment the biblical emphasis on the unity of personhood, help us better understanding the experience of granting forgiveness as a relief for our offender and as a relief even for us, and deepen our understanding of being embodied.

4.4 Virtuous behaviours – positive health effect?

Given the facts that forgiveness is good for our well-being the assumption may be obvious whether behaving in an virtuous way is a guarantee for mental and physical health. However this is not indisputable. People who had done good things, peacefully fought for freedom (such as Martin Luther), have been killed and that's doubtless no good health outcome. Others who engaged themselves for the poor, the sick and the suffering take on the burden of depression and grief or contract the illness of the people they serve. So being faithful and virtuous is no guarantee for physical and mental health. So it's not right to see mental well-being after forgiving as a gratification of God for our virtuous behaviour, it can be good for us to act virtuous but it can only be bad for us and our health. So I think we should not confuse God's gratification to us when we get into heaven with the gratification we get when forgiving has the effect of mental and physical well-being. But we shall be thankful, that

something like forgiveness exists and that it offers us the possibility to live together in peace
and harmony furthermore improve our health.

4.5 Greater health benefits for believers?

If the gospel message of the Christian religion tells us that forgiveness is a central aspect of
our human being then one might think that the positive effect of forgiveness on health is
higher with people who believe the gospel. The neuroscientist Jeeves tells that the basic
process of emotion, cognition, and physiology don't differ between Christians and non-
Christians. That may also be assumed for the matter of forgiveness. If forgiveness reduces
stress anxiety and anger in forgivers that will happen for Christians as well as for people with
different faiths. We all are human and we all function fundamentally in a same way. But it
may influence the effect of forgiveness that the meaning of forgiveness differs between
Christians and non-Christians. Because of the fact that the meaning of forgiveness may
influence the feelings, the thoughts and behaviour I think the forgiveness process of people
who see a religious meaning behind forgiveness may be faster completed than the one of
people without knowing that meaning and maybe the health effects are on a higher level too.

5 Personal Reflections on the matter of forgiveness

So we have learned a lot of forgiveness and health, we have answered questions that come up
to Christian eyes and minds if we see or hear something about empirical research of a matter
that is deeply Christian motivated and is a central perspective of our Scripture. I think it's a
good thing that medical and psychological science are interested in a matter of religion in that
way. Even though they are not really motivated by religious aspects I think it's important that
the do their researches, so we can see that psychology is a very important field for theologians
as well. Like we heard in our lecture it's a real pity that there are less professorships dealing
with psychological aspects of religion in Europe. I think it's an important field for progressive
and modern theologian inquiry. I think it should interest us much more what processes within
us human beings lead to religious thinking, which processes run within us while we have
religious feelings. On the matter of forgiveness I think psychology has found a way to show
that forgiving is something that could be good for us, especially for our health, but also for
peace. I can imagine that if psychologists would interact in wars and try to work with the
leadership of the hostile peoples with the focus on forgiveness intervention, it would be quite
easier to come together and to arrange a peaceful solution. I think the problem of today is that
there is so much hatred between the different peoples or religion (esp. in case of the Islamic
fundamentalists against the western peoples), that peaceful solutions are impossible to find

with conventional methods. I don't think that hatred is being reduced by applying sanctions
against the offended people and I think it would be useful to try a forgiveness intervention on
leaderships of hostile people. If the leaderships can forgive all the injustices then maybe the
hatred within the people will also have the chance to be reduced. I think forgiveness can be
useful for world peace. However, this shall be holding for the big wars and even for the little
wars like brawls against the neighbour, brawls within families, marital conflicts, child abuse,
and so on. I think forgiveness can help us to live our lives in peace and harmony. So I think
that it is important that empirical research finds out about the effects of forgiveness on
physical and mental health and that so people can see that forgiving is the right way to solve
their interpersonal differences. Christian communities shall go on promoting forgiveness in
their way and they shall see the empirical studies as a help to better understand the
phenomenon of forgiveness. Theologians shall not have fear that empirical forgiveness
research may make their inquiry needless but shall note the development on this sector with
interest and find ways to use results of empirical research for theological practice.

6 Bibliography

- **Subkoviak, Michael J. *et al***: Measuring forgiveness in late adolescence and middle
  adulthood, in: *Journal of Adolescence, 1995, 18, 641 - 655*

- **Grom, B.**: Forgiveness: die Bereitschaft zu vergeben. Ein aufstrebendes Thema
  psychologischer Beratung und Forschung, in: *Stimmen der Zeit, 220 (2002), 640-643*

- **VanOyen Witvliet, Charlotte**: Forgiveness and health: Review and Relflections on a
  Matter of Faith, Feelings and Physiology, in: *Journal of Psychology and Theology, 29
  (2001), 212 - 224*

- **Enright, Robert and Reed, Gale:** A process model of forgiving, in:
  http://www.forgiveness-institute.org/ifi/whatis/process_model_of_forgiving.html
  (fetched 04 February 2003)

LaVergne, TN USA
30 March 2011
222299LV00003B